Who is Nika Nikoubin?

A BLOODY LAS VEGAS HOTEL STORY

NIKA NIKOUBIN

Who is Nika Nikoubin?
A Bloody Las Vegas Hotel Story
Published by Nika Nikoubin

Copyright ©2023, NIKA NIKOUBIN LLC.
All rights reserved.

No part of this book may be reproduced in any form or by any mechanical means, including information storage and retrieval systems without permission in writing from the publisher/ author, except for the use of brief quotations in a book review. To request permissions, contact the publisher at
nikanikoubin55@gmail.com.
Editor: James C. Stanley

This publication is designed to provide accurate and authoritative information regarding the subject matter covered, and is the personal account of the author. All images, logos, quotes, and trademarks included in this book are subject to use according to trademark and copyright laws of the United States of America.

ISBN: 979-8-218-26706-3 (Paperback)
ISBN: 979-8-218-26707-0 (Ebook)
Library of Congress Control Number: 9798218179519

BIOGRAPHY & AUTOBIOGRAPHY / Criminals & Outlaws
BIOGRAPHY & AUTOBIOGRAPHY / Women

www.nikanikoubin.com

All rights reserved by NIKA NIKOUBIN.
This book is printed in the United States of America.

For Alexie!

thank you for you support :)

Niki

Nikmuli

Contents

Introduction 7

01 Early Life in Tehran 11
02 Coming to America: An Immigrant Girl's Life from Tehran, Iran to Lubbock, Texas. 31
03 College and Debate 53
04 Covid-19/Mental Health 69
05 What Happens in Vegas Doesn't Stay in Vegas ... 93
06 Custody Scene 127
07 Moving forward 149
08 Why did it happen again? 157
09 Future Plans/Conclusion 163

Introduction

"I need to call 911... I don't know what just happened. Am I in a movie? What's going on? I need to find someone to help me!" I thought to myself as I was hyperventilating and running unclothed aimlessly down the halls of a Las Vegas hotel. As I ran from the hotel room, I remember thinking, "Where am I?" I couldn't remember why I was running or why I was even in Las Vegas, let alone in some random hotel. Suddenly, two male police officers approached and started asking me strange questions. As the officers got closer, I could tell they had confused expressions on their faces as they stopped and stood unblinking, trying to process what they had just witness, while calling for assistance. I could hear them speaking however at this time everything is still a bit dreamy. I was thinking, "Why are they looking at me, what have I done, where am I?" I can hear the officers asking me "Ma'am do you need medical assistance?" However I was still unable to respond, as everything at this point is still a dream playing over and over in my head.

I can hear commotions going on around me as I come to my senses. "Oh, that's right I'm naked. Focus, Nika! Focus!" I couldn't believe it was real. I felt as though I was in a TV show watching myself. I could not comprehend exactly what the police officers were saying. I was just staring at them blankly. They were staring back at me. Everything was a blur and my mind was racing. I remember feeling very scared as these men were staring at me. I felt like a violated protagonist in a movie. It did not seem real.

The next day I was all over the news. Seeing my own mug shot gave me an out of body experience of despair that I had never experienced before. I didn't think it was real. It was hard to focus and set my mind on the smallest details of the nights before such as his name, what he had on, his eye color, what I was drinking, and what I actually did.

I'll try my best to go into detail about that night. I am more than what the headlines say. I am more than just a young girl who was struggling with mental health. I am more than a singer, student and artist. Like all human beings, I believe I am more than the sum of my parts. "It isn't the best picture the media is using," I thought as I watched myself on the news, feeling like my life was over. Here is my story:

Chapter 1:

Early Life in Tehran

In the summer of 2000, my parents welcomed the most precious joy to the world, Nika Nikoubin, born on May 31, 2000, in the exotic city of Tehran, Iran. Tehran, like with much of the culture of Iran, is often misunderstood and unknown to many not raised in the West. I was mostly raised in a small town in Texas. The small-town Texas environment provided me with great experiences, friends and perspective that allowed me to understand the dynamic intricacies of both Western and Persian culture.

Tehran is steeped in a rich and vibrant culture that spans centuries. Persian culture is a complex cornucopia of traditions, customs, and values that are layered over thousands of years. Tehran is derived from an old Persian word "Tiragan" which means "warm place." Tehran is a large, dynamic and vibrant city with a history that dates back to the 3rd millennium B.C. The Persian Empire, the Islamic Golden Age and the Safavid dynasty are just some of the layers that are still remnant in Persian culture today.

I was fully immersed in the rich art and culture of Tehran that would later inspire my deep love and interest in painting, poetry, music and architecture. Artists such as Rumi, Hafez, and Saadi are touchstones to Persian culture which encapsulate the deep expression of emotions and feelings captured in their poetry. As a young Persian girl, I often thought I would be able to sing the poetry they created.

Many of my friends in Texas, where we later moved, at no fault of their own, did not have a good understanding of Persian culture. From the mainstream movies such as *300: Rise of an Empire* to parodies on *South Park,* many did not understand the history of Iran or why the country is perceived so negatively in the West.

Iranian art and architecture are known for their attention to detail, intricate designs, and bright colors. The Golestan Palace and the Sheikh Latfollah Mosque are just a few of the many architectural marvels from Iran that I visited in person and continue to inspire my artistic expression. I began painting in elementary school and incorporated many of the design ques in my painting.

I grew up as an only child in a very loving and supportive family of academic parents who, from a young age, instilled the value of education in me. Like many girls who are raised in culturally conservative Iran, my parents were very strict and only allowed me to hang out with school friends if they approved and under their supervision. I didn't like the control, but I loved my parents. Despite this, I had a relatively happy and normal childhood.

My best friend while in Tehran was Elisa, who I met at my 6th birthday party when no one else showed up. Elisa and I would play with Barbie dolls. Like most typical six-year-old girls, Elisa and I would dress up our Barbies in different styles of fashion. Looking back now, much of my current interest in fashion stems from my playtime with Elisa. She would challenge my fashion sense and would push me to think outside of the box. However, later in my young life, my friendship with Elisa would come to an abrupt end as my mom was furthering her studies and was accepted to a master's program in a different city.

Both my mom and myself moved to Mashhad, Iran while my dad stayed back in Tehran to continue his work. It made me so sad to leave my father, but my mother would explain to me that it's necessary so we can all progress.

Life in Mashhad

When my mother got accepted for her master's program in Mashhad, I had to leave a very comfortable life in Tehran and move to Mashhad with just my mother. I missed my father greatly. As academics, my parents are very devoted to school and academia. My mother would explain to me the value of pursuing an education. I would write letters to my father about my life in Mashhad and he would come and visit us on weekends. It would make me so happy to see him. I remember writing to my dad about a loose tooth in my mouth because I thought he was friends with the Tooth Fairy and could therefore get her to come and visit me.

Life was difficult in Mashhad because I missed my dad dearly. I had to adjust to a new life in a different environment while making new friends and getting familiar with my new city and surroundings. My mother was devoted to her studies and taking care of me, but I really wanted my father to be with us. When I moved to Mashhad, I started first grade and made some friends. I did not wear the hijab until later in life as culturally, young Iranian girls are not required to wear it even though the practice is still observed by most students. Not wearing the hijab would sometimes lead to students bullying, but I wanted freedom.

I loved chocolate milk and indulged in that simple treat almost every day before going to school. I chose to sit near the window in class so I could see my mother the second she arrived to pick me up. Seeing her beautiful smile as she picked me up made my day. No matter how bad or how hard school was becoming, I knew she would always be there for me and accept me for who I am. My mother made me feel happy about myself as she loved me so much.

During this time in my life, my talents in the arts started to accelerate and get noticed by both my peers and teachers. I began participating and excelling in handwriting, drawing and painting competitions. Despite my parents not being overly religious, I had an excellent memory and even memorized the Quran as a first grader. I continued to achieve high marks in school, despite the abrupt move to a different school and city.

I remember this time as being the beginning of my love for the arts and gaining a deeper understanding of culture as Mashhad contrasted with Tehran in so many ways. The change in city and environment helped me compare and contrast different cultures. It would later help me to better understand and appreciate the United States.

One of the most memorable aspects of Mashhad was the excellent food. Mashhad is known for food, and the kabobs and ghormeh sabzi are some of the best Persian dishes I have ever experienced in my life. Pesaran Karim was one of my favorite restaurants in the world. I have yet to find a Persian restaurant in America, or any place in the world for that matter, that could match the way Persaran Karim makes its lamb kebabs.

Returning to Tehran

After my mother completed her master's program, we returned to Tehran to rejoin my father. As I mentioned before, my parents were not very religious so I did not start wearing the hijab until fifth grade, which is considered late in Iran. This caused me to receive some bullying from other students who religiously wore the hijab and whose families were stricter. I attended a different school every year, including a prestigious, private middle school called the Rabbani Institute of Culture and Education in Tehran.

The Rabbani Institute is a well-known school with a very low acceptance rate and challenging curriculum. In order to enroll in the school, I had to score in the top two of all entrance exam takers to gain admission. It was a very challenging school, but in a good way. When I moved to America, I was well prepared to succeed in the Texas public school system. During my time at the Rabbani School, I met one of my dearest friends, Nazanin. She was a talented and gifted student. Nazanin and I would engage in the usual mischievous endeavors such as sneaking into class and playing tricks on one another. We couldn't really do anything too mischievously drastic as school in Iran and particularly at the Rabbani School, was extremely challenging. We had to pay attention, follow the instructions of teachers and generally work very hard as it was easy to fall behind on work as many in my peer group were successful high achievers.

Talents in Music and Choir

As my artistic tendencies started to blossom, my parents additionally enrolled me in a specialized music school, where I learned to play the flute, violin, and took singing classes. My teachers and parents identified my natural talent for music and helped me become skilled in playing musical instruments along with improving my singing range. Singing was really cathartic. I was so glad to be in the music school.

In 5th grade, I auditioned for the choir and was selected to join. Although my parents were hesitant at first, one of my teachers convinced them that it would be a great opportunity for me to be part of the school choir. The year I joined, we won first place in all of Tehran for the best performance. Expressing oneself through their voice is so human. I am so thankful that I was afforded all of these opportunities to explore and express myself artistically, even from a young age. To this day, the arts are what I lean on when I'm feeling down or lost. In fact, it is what I was doing when I took the turn to Las Vegas.

Pets and Other Hobbies

Apart from my musical and artistic hobbies, I also had a unique playmate named

Aristotle. Aristotle took up a lot of my time as most playtime with other students was so regulated. He was my friend. Let me tell you that Aristotle was the smartest rooster I have ever encountered. He was fun and playful. It's amazing how people and animals connect. I enjoyed playing and caring for Aristotle and my other chickens.

Having chickens is probably not as common in the United States, but roosters and chickens are smart animals. I connected with them, as traditionally in Iran, dogs aren't normally considered house pets. At a young age, Aristotle instilled in me a deep love for pets that extended beyond roosters and later to dogs and cats when I moved to the U.S.

I also participated in athletic activities such as competitive speed skating, basketball and other sports. I liked sports. Like music, sports afforded me the opportunity to work with teammates towards a common goal.

I participated in numerous sports camps in Tehran during summer time and even won the gold medal in my division for speed skating. In later years, I would follow my passion for sports by participating in indoor cycling.

Family in Iran

I had a very close family living in Iran, including close uncles and aunts in Isfahan. I also had an uncle that lived in the city of Shomal. Shomal was very beautiful as it was close to the ocean, and although clothing was strict in Iran, I could still relax at the beach with appropriate clothing. My uncle owned a couple of local restaurants and was a successful businessman. He would always welcome our family to his house and restaurants for family gatherings. I can remember these moments as we gathered and enjoyed the taste of the Shomal Koloocheh cookies we would eat during this time.

My grandmother and my other aunt lived in Kermanshah. My mom's side of the family are Kurdish in ethnicity. Kurds are an ethnic group who live throughout the Middle East. In Iran, Kurds are a minority group that speak Kurmanji, Sorani, and other Kurdish dialects. They have other distinct cultural practices related to food, clothing, dance, and music. Kurds are a significant part of Iranian culture, having contributed in so many ways. Mohammad Hossein Shahriar and Ahmad Aram are just a few of the writers and poets who have contributed significantly to Persian culture.

Being raised in this juxtaposition of culture, I started to understand the cultural layers that make Iran such a rich culture and how it influences my perspective in life. The geography of the city was absolutely amazing with its great mountains and mild California- like weather. I had an aunt who owned a pharmacy store in the city. She had a pet cat that I always played with. I also loved my grandparents' house. I would always "steal" candy from the living room cabinet, but just like most loving grandparents' they enjoyed my childish mischief and were happy they could give me treats without my parents knowing.

My dad's side of the family resided in the city of Isfahan. I loved Isfahan's culture. My uncles and aunts there were so kind and loving. They would always treat us to fun family parties with such wonderful food. They owned businesses in the city and worked for banks. At family parties in Isfahan, we would traditionally eat on the floor while my uncles challenged me with all sorts of math problems and trivia questions. I would also play video games with my family friends there.

I had a very happy childhood with my close family, and through them my love for education and the arts was fostered from a young age. I had a unique upbringing, moving from Tehran to Mashhad and back, attending different schools every year, while having a pet rooster named Aristotle. During this time, my propensity towards music and love for pets flourished. I felt loved.

Chapter 2:

Coming to America: An Immigrant Girl's Life from Tehran, Iran to Lubbock, Texas.

My parents were excelling in their academic careers, and this was at a time when Iran was facing some of the biggest protests for freedom from the oppressive Iranian regime. The Green Movement, or the Persian Awakening, was a major political and social event in Iran. In 2009, Iran held an election that was marred by allegations of fraud and voting irregularities. Both candidates claimed the other had rigged the election, and on the ground level, the people became restless as government officials continued to debate who won the election. I was only eight at the time, but I remember experiencing the palpable emotions of the Green Movement and seeing people's passion in the streets with their peace signs, and chants for freedom while wearing green.

The United States had always been a dream destination for my family, and when we finally got the opportunity to move there, we were more than thrilled. We felt as if we had won the lottery. We loved America and what it stood for: Freedom. It was always the dream of so many Iranians to be able to move to the United States and experience true freedom away from an oppressive government.

We fantasized about the freedoms enjoyed by U.S. citizens and the endless possibilities and opportunities for tremendous growth. Getting to live our life to the fullest potential as human beings was a dream we could only imagine in Iran. When my family announced that we would be moving to the U.S. all our friends and family congratulated us and were happy that we could expand upon our opportunities in a way that the Iranian government wouldn't have allowed.

The process of getting to the U.S. was a long and tedious one, but we were all determined to make it there. My mother studied for English language exams and we processed for our visa interviews in Ankara, Turkey, before finally getting our visas to come to the United States. I remember the journey to the U.S. being so long. We flew from Iran to Dubai and then to Dallas, before finally ending in Lubbock. Along the way, I remember thinking that I'll be so happy to finally be in our dream land of the United States.

The first time I set foot in the U.S. however, I was surprised to find it different from what I had imagined. Everything was so flat and barren. I remember when we first arrived in Lubbock, Texas I asked my mother, "Is this really the United States everyone talks about?"

I later realized it was because Lubbock was a small city compared to bigger cities such as New York or Dallas. It felt like a small village, but I later appreciated the charm of growing up in a small Texas town.

It was one of the longest travel journeys I have ever experienced in my young life. We moved to Lubbock because we had close family that had lived there for years. My father got a teaching and research position at Texas Tech University while my studious mother pursued her Ph.D. at the same university. I started attending Friendship Heritage Middle School.

School in Lubbock

Middle school was an entirely new experience for me, and I had to adjust to many new things, including the English language and the new culture. I carried a dictionary with me everywhere I went and relied on friends to help me better learn English. The school also had an ESL program, where I made a good friend named Tori, who befriended me as we were both learning English.

Although I had studied English in Iran, keeping up with the fast-paced learning in America was challenging. I also faced some bullying because I did not know about American beauty standards, like shaving my legs and doing my eyebrows. At this time I started to develop low self-esteem and insecurities.

I faced even more culture shocks when I started attending a co-ed school for the first time. I had never been around boys like this. Seeing a classmate get pregnant in the seventh grade was shocking to me. At this point, I had no idea what sex even meant. Guys were intimidating, and I did not know how to act around them. I was shy and scared of them. After a year at Friendship Heritage Middle School, I accelerated to Talkington High School for Women, one of Texas's top-performing magnet schools. I was extremely shy as this was all still so new to me, and adjusting to high school took some time. I was a nerd. I was studious and became more confident in my English skills at high school.

I started to make close friends while participating in different extracurricular activities. I even ran for class president and won! I remember feeling so good about myself at that moment. "I did it! I was given a chance, I worked hard and made it! This is the American Dream!" I was on top of the world!

This win inspired me to participate in other competitions such as math and science contests, debate clubs and volunteering for the Make-A-Wish Foundation. I also became part of the school government, a cheerleader, and a school dancer. I ended up becoming the typical all-American high school student in sports-centered Lubbock, Texas.

I didn't initially understand American football, but I soon found myself enamored with the athletic boys who would smash their heads into others and the excitement of Friday night lights in Lubbock. In Texas, football is king, I learned that very quickly living there.

While in Student Congress, I became friends with a girl named Skyler during my junior year. We remained friends throughout college and to this day, despite all that has happened, she has been a constant source of support and unconditional love in my life.

I rebelled against my parents for the first time when I told them I was taking an extra class at a different high school. At this other school, I had the chance to hang out with my first boyfriend. We later broke up because we couldn't see each other as much as we wanted.

I also had my first job at this time and worked hard. I was a top scholar and graduated third in my class. I even had the opportunity to give my class commencement speech at graduation. I delivered the speech and used quotes from Bill Hybels: "Storms draw something out of us that calm seas don't." In the later chapters of my book, I will go into detail about some of my experiences and the storms that altered my life forever.

During high school, I remained an avid member of the choir and twice won first place in solo and ensemble competitions. I even sang at Texas Tech University for the New Year's celebration. I loved making my parents proud. I loved seeing their smiling faces as I excelled in my young life. Despite all this, I was still struggling with many things, such as understanding boys, my weight, as well as my mental health and self-esteem. It was a facade to me, it was an enigma.

The summer before my freshman year at college was an extremely difficult time for me. Unfortunately, I experienced a traumatic sexual experience that made me feel both extreme shame while lowering my self-esteem and self-worth even further in the process. I felt terrible all the time and all my insecurities were exasperated. I didn't know what to do. I would have anxiety attacks and cry uncontrollably in the bathroom by myself, hoping no one would hear me.

Coming from Persian culture, talking about subjects like sexual trauma is very taboo, but I want to be open about my experiences to enable more women to recover from their own trauma if they've had a similar experience.

I also kept this subject a secret from my parents and because of the shame, I didn't even seek counseling. I started to hallucinate and would see my violator everywhere on campus. I would see his face and eyes on people as I walked past them. It was like a horror film with zombies all around me wearing his face as their mask. I would have random panic and anxiety attacks. I blamed myself for it all. I was really depressed and sad, and didn't know how to cope with it.

I needed to get out of Lubbock. I needed the hallucinations to stop. I resorted to eating excessive amounts of food to deal with the emotions. I was overweight and depressed. Thankfully, I had good friends that were like a life saving support system for me. Skyler and Tawny were two close friends from high school who comforted me and were there to listen when I needed someone to talk to.

I couldn't talk to my parents though. There was just too much shame attached. I hated what that boy had done to me. I'm not a victim. I will and have overcome a lot from that bad experience. I had flashbacks to the incident when I started to lose control that night in Las Vegas.

While I hate the experience, I know that it will ultimately make me a better person.

I won't let it rob me of who I am. I won't let it hold me down from reaching who I know I am.

Freshman year at College

As I started school at Texas Tech University, I began college as a Public Relations major. I would later discover that this degree would be a great help with my situation of dealing with the media.

However, I did not find the major as engaging as I liked so I started exploring other areas of study. I really enjoyed my ethics class which was a humanities requirement for freshman. I fell in love with philosophy.

I would later change my major to philosophy in the spring semester of that year. I really enjoyed my philosophy courses. I liked the way the professors would push our minds to discuss and debate ideas such as existentialism, philosophy of emotions or Descarte's "evil demon" problem and how it related to a modern film like The Matrix. Studying philosophy was an escape for me. I began to engross my mind into my studies while ignoring and burying the issues related to my sexual trauma.

I also joined the Texas Tech debate team. I loved debate in high school and was excited to continue my journey into college level debate. As I already mentioned, I am a nerd. I had, and continue to have, the goal of practicing law and viewed debate as being good practice for my desired profession.

Although the coaches and staff of the team were very helpful and supportive, like many teams we had a lot of drama. I never really felt like I was on a "team" and always felt this competitive energy around my fellow members. I felt like I was a character on the Gossip Girl television show rather than a member of an educational debate team. I didn't feel accepted. I didn't feel happy. I felt left out.

Oftentimes at debate competitions, I found more camaraderie with the opposing teams and would later become friends with many of my competitors.

I became acquainted with one of the top programs in the U.S., the Parliamentary Debate at Berkeley. Unlike Texas Tech, the Parliamentary Debate at Berkeley treated me with so much kindness and acceptance. I felt a sincere friendship and connection with the members of the Berkeley team. Although many of my own Texas Tech teammates gossiped about me spilling secret information to the Berkeley team, I in fact never traded any secrets. I learned a lot from their team and appreciated their friendship. I also had a crush on one of the members who I would later go on to date.

In the fall of 2018, there was an important debate competition I had to attend but my parents had already bought tickets for us to visit family in Iran. However, this trip to Iran conflicted with one of the more important debate tournaments. I rebelled and stayed at the Berkeley teams' house while my parents ended up flying to Iran by themselves.

During this time I got to learn more about debate and the Berkeley team. An added benefit was that I was with the boy who I had a crush on. Like any young girl, I was drawn by my emotions to this guy.

Summer 2019

Although I faced a lot of challenges in Lubbock, especially after graduating high school, I was still determined to live my best life. I found comfort in food, which led to significant weight gain. Spring semester of college saw me becoming determined to break out of my depression and change my bad habits. I started going to the recreation center and also re-started my habit of exercising regularly. But I just couldn't get myself into a routine with any activities such as weight lifting.

I did, however, find joy in indoor cycling. In fact, spin class became my passion. At an early age, I indulged in adrenaline sports such as speed skating and basketball. Indoor cycling provided me with an escape and a similar adrenaline rush. It also helped that many spin classes revolve around great music and enthusiastic coaches. It was a real escape from my negative feelings.

In the Summer of 2019, I discovered Fitness studio, which is a spin chain with locations all over the country. Fitness studio Lubbock soon became my home away from home. The classes were much more challenging than the fitness classes offered at the recreation center at my school, and I reveled in the challenge.

I remember taking my first class at Fitness studio Lubbock and falling in love with the experience on the first try. The motivating music and thrill of an enthusiastic instructor would push me to become the best version of myself. My self-esteem was starting to rebuild. I was feeling motivated and far happier.

I would later take my mom and my dad for mothers and fathers day at Fitness studio where they were able to feel the magic I felt while riding at those classes. With the combination of intermittent fasting and taking two Fitness studio classes daily, I was able to lose nearly fifty pounds in three months. I was proud of myself. Not only did I lose the weight gained during my freshman year, but I also now had toned muscles and felt a better sense of well-being.

I became part of the Fitness studio family and continued to be a part of it for the next two years at various locations around the country. I was even employed at Fitness studio in Berkeley, CA when I moved to California and also worked for them in Texas.

Overall, my journey as an immigrant in America has been filled with some challenges, but I have also had the opportunity to have wonderful experiences that have helped me grow and understand how wonderful it is to live in the United States.

Chapter 3:

College and Debate

I was an accomplished debater in high school, and continuing my college journey was very exciting. Debate was one of my favorite activities to participate in at college. Although I did not attend the national competition in debate during my freshman year at Texas Tech University, I was eventually able to transfer to Berkeley City College, and the UC Berkeley student organization debate team, Parliamentary debate at Berkeley, accepted me with open arms to participate in their team.

Moving to Berkeley, CA

Moving from Lubbock, TX, to Berkeley, CA, was one of the most exciting things that happened in my life. Not only was I able to gain employment and housing before I moved to California, but I was also invited to join one of the top debate programs in the country. Compared to the flat city of Lubbock, I loved Berkeley. The rolling hills and mild temperatures were the exact opposite of my experience in Lubbock. Lubbock is a special place in its own way, but Berkeley felt like a glove to me.

I loved walking throughout the town and the ups and downs of the city's hills. I did not have a driver's license, let alone a car, but I was determined to explore the city and walked everywhere.

When walking from my debate fraternity house to my work at Fitness studio Berkeley then to the UC Berkeley campus, I would experience and encounter so many different happy people. Whether it be a local shopkeeper or the regular homeless man who would smile and wave, Berkeley at that time had a magical, happy feeling of community.

Moving was not easy or cheap. I was given a room in a debate fraternity house where most of the Berkeley Parliamentary Debate team lived. My rent was relatively cheap compared to what most people would pay to live in Berkeley, but I also had to deal with living in a house with twenty other young people. I had my own private room, and the house had four floors and a basement. It was often loud, and there wasn't much privacy.

I did, however, love all my roommates at the house. Everything in Berkeley seemed as though it was the exact opposite of Lubbock. It was an enigma to me. It was exactly what I was seeking to be exposed to the world and learn about it through experiences.

Berkeley's open acceptance and culture drew me in as an immigrant philosophy student who often viewed the world differently. I loved living in Berkley. My days would consist of leaving the debate house in the morning, going to school, working at Fitness studio, hanging around the city, and finishing up with studying and debate practice at night. From living in Berkley, I was exposed to everything from cryotherapy to veganism.

The Debate Team at Berkeley

Being a part of the Berkeley debate team was one of my best "team" experiences. Being amongst top debaters who accepted me helped challenge me to work harder than ever. This team was also student-run which provided more autonomy from other administratively structured teams. The Berkley team was very cohesive, and team members continued to push me to work on my debates for hours while enjoying the sincere friendship they offered.

It's challenging to describe college debate to those who may be more prone to watching a college football or basketball game. However, debate is actually similar to those sports, albeit in an academic way. The mechanics of the National Parliamentary Debate Association (NPDA) assigned both competing teams an affirmative or negative side of an issue. Then a topic will be provided, and both teams have twenty minutes to prepare for the debate round. The opposing team members then engage in an engrossing and uniform-speech patterned debate about the shared topic raising and discounting opposing viewpoints.

One can run many types of arguments in an NPDA debate round, including theories, criticisms, disadvantages, advantages, impacts, etc. If you're unfamiliar with the debate rules, often the affirmative side could reject the topic and run a "criticism." This is like running a "trick play" in athletic team sports such as football. This "criticism" can come in multiple forms and use numerous reasons for grounds to cite it. The criticisms could include reasoning that the topic is too problematic or not critical or that the topic is not relevant to anything related to the debate.

I excelled as both a competitor and teammate as I really found a groove with my teammates. Amanda, my teammate and partner, and myself, placed 3rd at the national Round Robin competition in 2019. I ultimately did not participate in other national competitions, but I still felt fulfilled by my small successes in debate. It was helping me repair myself from my trauma. I was starting to feel like I could be whole again. I felt as though I was growing.

College in Berkeley

I proceeded through school at Berkeley City College, my parents expressed to me that I needed to attend a university to challenge myself. I knew that after one year at community college, I would be able to transfer to a U.C. California school. I maintained a perfect G.P.A. at Berkeley City College while participating in the Parliamentary Debate team and working part-time at Fitness studio.

Like my parents, I enjoy school and academia. I connected with all of my professors who were very supportive of my participation in debate and other groups while on campus. I felt accepted and I had many friends in school. It was exactly what I dreamed college was about.

I also enjoyed much of Berkley's food. From Telegraph to the "gourmet ghetto," Berkeley had endless food options. Rojbas Grill was one of my favorite places to indulge in some wonderful salmon kebab while Butcher's Son provided me with satisfaction for my love of bagels.

Dating in Berkeley

I also started to date one of the Berkeley team members. He was kind, brilliant, funny, and enjoyable to be around. He was nothing like my transgressor. When I first landed at Berkeley, he picked me up and surprised me with roses. I felt special. I had a fun time dating him then, but things don't always work out the perfect way you imagine when you're young and in love. I had this perfectionist idea of a "perfect relationship." There were so many ups and downs in the relationship, and even though I felt a lot of love, I would sometimes be left feeling betrayed. I am forever grateful for the countless hours we spent together, working on our debate skills, and for allowing me to stay with his loving parents when I decided to stay back for the debate competition.

Although I had a lot of friends from school and the debate team, I wanted to continue to include more friends in my life. I opened an account on dating apps, such as Tinder, to meet new people and friends. I was always keen to meet people who could provide mentorship about college and career or expand my horizons for success. I met many people from these apps, even if it was just for grabbing ice cream or coffee and having a conversation.

Dimas was one of the men I remember meeting during this time. Dimas was born and raised in Russia. Dimas was older, and would challenge my thinking unlike the boys I had been dating before.

His philosophy in life consists of pure energy, meditation, and yoga, as well as staying clear of all enhancements, including all medications, alcohol, drugs or even caffeine. After meeting him, I enrolled at Yoga Tree in Oakland and participated in multiple yoga sessions that lasted almost three hours each session.

It was my friendship with Dimas that prompted me to later refuse taking medications which would, later on, lead to that night in Las Vegas. It was my choice to follow this philosophy but his advice wouldn't turn out to be the best for someone who struggles with diagnosed bipolar and schizophrenia like myself and therefore needs medication to stabilize. I didn't know what I was going through at the time. I just knew I didn't feel in control and would feel extremes.

Fitness studio Berkeley

I loved working at Fitness studio Berkeley. I was blessed to be hired before I even moved to Berkeley and made friends with one of the managers named Lauren. Lauren introduced me to the best coffee in Berkeley. I continued my love of Fitness studio in Berkeley and would take classes daily. I had a healthy supportive friendship with my co-workers and wanted to be the top sales employee, which I managed to achieve for several months. I fell in love with all aspects of the sport and participated in numerous bike festivals around the city.

Although my job was concentrated on sales and studio maintenance, I had goals and ambitions to become a manager or a cycling instructor at Fitness studio. However, my full-time school and debate work made it difficult to fully pursue a management role. As I worked hard at Fitness studio, I thought to myself, "If I work here for a year, I'm sure I will eventually achieve a managerial role in the future."

I would later achieve my ambitions and become a manager of Fitness studio in Texas, but my mental health struggles were just beginning when I worked there. I would later lose control of who I am which lead to that night in a Las Vegas hotel.

Chapter 4:

Covid-19/ Mental Health

Living in Berkeley, CA, was one of the most enjoyable times of my educational experiences. I experienced being relatively independent from my parents—living on my own, working, going to school, and participating in extracurricular activities. However, the fun came to a sudden end when the Covid-19 pandemic hit the world.

In March 2020, I was participating at a debate competition in Missouri when the pandemic started to effect things in America. At first, I did not believe what was happening. Everything was closing down so suddenly. Then all of a sudden, in the middle of the competition, my parents called and told me that I needed to come back home.

I thought to myself, "Where is home though?" Berkeley was my home because I finally started to feel independent and loved being independent, however, my parents wanted me to return to live with them as the pandemic ravaged the country. While I was living in Berkeley, CA, my dad lived in an apartment in Dallas as he was offered a position at the University of Texas at Dallas. He wanted our family to move to Dallas as at that time my mom was staying in Lubbock. During the pandemic, my mother would move back to the Dallas area and find a position at a Dallas research institute, rejoining my dad.

After the competition ended, I flew to Dallas even though all of my possessions remained in Berkeley. At the time, my parents still had not purchased a home and were living in the one-bedroom apartment that my dad was renting. I moved back. I was scared. My parents were scared and the world suddenly closed down.

The One-bedroom apartment in Dallas, TX

After my experience living in Berkley, living in a one-bedroom apartment with my parents while the pandemic started was not ideal. Everything was closed or closing and everyone was scared. Everyone started to wear masks and wash their hands excessively. My hands hurt from how many times I would wash them. I started to feel confined. I started to feel controlled. I was panicking inside. My mental health struggles were increasing excessively at this time. I needed to see someone, but it was impossible as the world was shut down.

I missed the pre-pandemic days at Berkeley so much. I missed working out every day at Fitness studio and being around my friends, working, and attending school. I missed the routine. I became severely depressed because my online classes were dull and I missed the connections with my friends. I hated using Zoom. I just couldn't pay attention. I felt like I had severe ADHD as I took my classes. I started to feel disconnected. I started to get more depressed.

I would later ask my parents to help me purchase an fitness bike, and I started to get back on my exercise regime. It was difficult initially as I was used to the environment of Fitness studio with mood lights, motivating music and an enthusiastic instructor. I did my best and even became my own instructor by formatting and planning out my own workout routines. I wanted to become an fitness instructor, so it was the perfect chance to build upon my skills and to cope with my depression.

Cycling also helped rekindle some of my old passion for art and music. I started to paint again. It was a release. I painted a beautiful tiger to represent my spiritual animal of hard work and dedication. Those are some of the tenets I lived my life with. I loved doing acrylic paintings as it gave me a sense of purpose. I could listen to music and work on my art for hours without getting tired. I was hypnotized by art. I was engrossed in the process.

My hobbies allowed me to cope with a dark time in my life. Myself, like others my age, endured a trying time during very formative years. Being a young 20-year-old during the pandemic was not fun.

Mental Health and Therapy

Although I was able to do art and workout, my depression started to get worse when I lost the routine I had living in California. I could no longer go to work, walk around the city, and hang out with my close group of friends. I also started to have flashbacks to my past sexual trauma. I felt suffocated. I didn't feel in control. I felt as though I was going backwards in life. I did not have any peers, friends or close relationships when I moved back to Dallas.

My hallucinations started to come back, and I would see my violator everywhere. I cried every night and would endure uncontrolled flashbacks at night. I consistently had nightmares about the incident. I think this was because I had never dealt with the underlying issues. I was still ashamed. I still couldn't tell my parents about it. It still made me feel bad about myself. For a very long time, I continued to blame myself.

When I was living with my parents, I finally disclosed my sexual trauma incident to them. I needed someone to talk to, and they were very supportive of me. They showed more understanding than I assumed they would as Persian culture is very conservative and reserved when it comes to sexual topics. My parents recommended that I have therapy, and for the first time, I started seeking help and treatment for the incident.

I don't believe that online therapy is always the most effective; however, there were only so many options at the time that I could find. Most therapists were booked and not accepting new clients as many were struggling and the mental health system had become overwhelmed. In my online therapy sessions, I participated in Eye Movement Desensitization and Reprocessing (EMDR) treatment for my PTSD as well as Cognitive Behavioral Therapy (CBT) for my depression. My therapist was a good doctor, and I was happy that I was finally in treatment; however, I resisted taking anti-depression or mood stabilizers as I thought therapy was enough. I believed in the philosophy that my body has all it needs and after talking to others on these drugs, I did not want to take anything that would numb my creative and athletic desires.

Return to Berkeley, CA

As the pandemic year started to come to an end, some of the lockdowns were lifted and more businesses started to open back up. I asked my parents if I could return to Berkeley. Although they were worried about my health, the pandemic seemed to have subsided, and being the supportive types, they allowed me to return to Berkeley to finish my entire year in California. Flying from Dallas to Oakland during the pandemic was very strange. The airports were empty, and I felt like I was on a private plane as it was mostly empty. California was still on full lockdown. Everything was closed. It wasn't the same.

I returned to the fraternity debate house I was living in before. I started cooking and hiking a lot more. Even though Berkeley was not the same with the pandemic, I was happy to be back. Fitness studio Berkeley opened under numerous COVID safety protocols. The world really had changed.

I got to see my debate friends again and discuss the pandemic. It seemed as though we were all struggling because of it. The fear, the closings, the general lack of socializing with others.

I continued my online therapy in California as I wanted to keep improving and to heal. I completed my entire year at Berkeley. I also was notified that all colleges would be online due to the pandemic. After that, I had to go back to Dallas.

Return to Dallas, TX

I filled out my California taxes and thought I was considered a California resident. Right before leaving to go back to Dallas, I got the news I was hoping for:

"Ms. Nikoubin, you have been accepted to the University of California Los Angeles as an in-state tuition student!"

This was my dream school. At the time, UCLA was ranked the number one college in America in U.S. News university rankings. I was so happy. I felt all my hard work and dedication was paying off.

I was waitlisted to UCLA as a high school applicant, and it was very rewarding to finally be accepted to this highly revered school I always dreamed of attending. My parents, as academics, were so proud of my acceptance. Initially, I was accepted with the bonus of an in-state tuition rate since I had lived in California for more than a year. I thought I had finally achieved what I set my mind to when I first moved to California.

However, UCLA later changed the in-state tuition decision which shocked both my parents and myself. I tried appealing the decision, but was given no choice but to accept my offer as an out-of-state student and pay a very high tuition. As you might already know, college is expensive.

This change in tuition would later lead to me dropping out of UCLA as I could not afford the non-resident student rates and was unable to get loans. This had a significant impact on my mental health. UCLA was a dream achievement. I had worked hard to make it there, but in the end, was not able to afford my senior year to graduate.

This was very frustrating for me. I truly believe in my heart that if I stayed in school, I wouldn't have gotten in trouble, and the Las Vegas incident wouldn't have happened. More than anything, I was incredibly disappointed in myself, that I couldn't finish what I started.

Even though I accepted my offer to become a UCLA student, I was disappointed to learn that even with the expensive tuition, all my classes would be held online. This meant I could not attend the beautiful campus, make friends, and had to participate in class through a computer screen. The world had changed. I was changing with it. My depression grew deeper and I started to act out. I was stuck in Texas and attending UCLA online. It wasn't ideal, but I kept going, ignoring my mental health and pushing forward. However, I was about to break.

Life in Frisco, TX

Even though the pandemic was still ongoing and the closing and openings of states would see-saw, more businesses in Texas started to open up. In the spring of 2021, my parents found and purchased a home, and we moved from the one-bedroom apartment to our new spacious home. We had enough space for the three of us. I loved my new room and house. I even painted my room a light pink color to personalize it to my theme.

I had mixed feelings when I started school at UCLA. Since it was online, some of the positives meant that I could study and participate in school from the comfort of my home. I participated in all my classes, joined the sorority Kappa Delta, while trying my best to socialize with my fellow students. But it wasn't the same. I felt disconnected. I was depressed and growing deeper into my sadness. I enjoyed UCLA online as much as I could, but I was unable to join the debate team as UCLA did not have a NPDA debate team. From being so disconnected and isolated in Dallas, I started to have a lot of nervous energy. So to try and counter that I thought, "Why not create an NPDA debate team at UCLA?"

I learned a lot while participating in the student-run organization and Parliamentary Debate at U.C. Berkeley. I had the knowledge and experience of a student-run team. So, I decided I would utilize my leadership skills to become the Director of Forensics (DOF) for the team.

I then started the NPDA debate team at UCLA, known as Bruins@NPDA. I recruited over one hundred students for the team and two coaches who held multiple national championship records. I had a lot of experience under my belt, from placing in national competitions to being a part of two of the top debate programs in the country. I implemented what I learned from my experiences and formed a successfully run team at UCLA.

Despite my experience, I sometimes felt intimidated at national meetings, knowing that I was the youngest D.O.F. there. But I did not let that hold me back from assuring the team's success. That year the team placed fifth place in the sweepstakes ranking of all national teams for participating and collecting points at national-prep tournaments. I am forever grateful for the assistance the coaches provided for the team and was happy that I could create a social space for students in similar situations of having to complete school online.

I also started working at Fitness studio Frisco. I loved returning to Cycelbar studios and exercising. Fitness studio Frsico was a modern and classy space. I loved the level of professionalism that they encouraged at work. I started as the sales associate and I would, later on, train to become an instructor at that studio with the assistance of my amazing instructor, Berniece.

Social Life

Although I was happy to live in Texas, at my parents' nice home, I still missed my friends and the network of connections I had made all over the country through debate. I felt very alone and isolated in Texas, so I started to use Bumble BFF to find friends to socialize with. I met some great girls from the app and it helped with releasing some of the suffocation I was feeling as a result of the pandemic. This was the beginning of me using these apps to meet people. This would later lead to the trouble I experienced in Las Vegas.

Skyler, my high school friend, would try her best to visit me when she could. She could tell something was wrong. She seemed to know that I wasn't the same happy girl she had grown up with. We would go out to socialize, and I started to drink. I had never drank alcohol before. But I felt isolated and alone, and it seemed to help.

I met Ella on one of these nights out. Ella was very nice and would hang out with me throughout the week as she lived nearby. She helped me with my loneliness as we connected instantly.

I traveled to Las Vegas with Skyler and Ella for my twenty-first birthday. This was my first time going to Vegas. The trip was thrilling and exciting to a level I can't describe. We even stayed at the Cosmopolitan Hotel.

We were all twenty-one, so we went out every night to explore and enjoy all that

Las Vegas had to offer. It was alluring. It truly never slept. We certainly never slept. Las Vegas had my heart. I was depressed I would not be able to continue at UCLA and I wanted something to make me feel better. Las Vegas was my medicine. As the summer went on I fell deeper into my despair.

December 2021

By December 2021, I was beginning to spiral. My mental health was not in a good place. I couldn't control it. It began to significantly decline. Retrospectively, this was the beginning of the events that lead to my arrest in March 2022 in Las Vegas.

In January, I purchased a one way ticket to Los Angeles to see one of my ex-boy-friends. I was not in the right mind. I was so depressed. I remember being obsessed with death at the time. I was hallucinating, and I was drinking and taking anything that anyone would offer me just to escape.

The relationship we had for the few days I stayed at his place did not make sense, and I remember him calling me "crazy," which upset me. I would later leave his place and visit a relative who lived in Orange County.

While at my relatives house, I had multiple manic and hallucination episodes. At one point, I believed everyone was trying to poison me and I started yelling out about it. I would cry uncontrollably, I would have panic attacks. I just couldn't control it.

I would later return to Dallas. I felt angry, sad and completely disconnected from reality. I don't remember much about it, but I got in a fight with my loving parents at the time. I had to be sequestered at a mental hospital. I ended up being there for ten days in the end. It helped, but my hallucinations were getting stronger on the medicines I was provided. I couldn't control what was happening. I felt as though I was losing my mind. So, this time I bought a one way ticket to Las Vegas.

Chapter 5:

What Happens in Vegas Doesn't Stay in Vegas

I loved being in Las Vegas. Compared to being in Lubbock or Dallas, Las Vegas had a vibe I had not lived in before. It was my second time in the city and all I thought about was how the place seemed true. I had dropped out of college and was depressed. I was lost and my mental health had severely degraded. I was trying to be happy, but couldn't achieve it.

I had close friends from Lubbok living in Las Vegas, so it was a great place to jump-start my next endeavor, my music career. I roomed with my friend Holly and embarked on my musical journey.

Looking back retrospectively, I was not in my right mind. I had left Dallas suddenly. I didn't even tell my parents I was leaving until the night before my flight. I had already bought my ticket and decided to leave for Vegas with or without their approval. I was on medication that seemed to dull my senses rather than allow me to experience anything. I hated the medications and how they made me feel.

In Las Vegas, I was drawn to the city. I was drawn to the entertainers who were there and the ones from the past who made it there. Brittany Spears, Jennifer Lopez, and Elton John were just a few of the performers I thought about as I walked the Las Vegas strip, while thinking about how I would pursue my own music career and journey.

I was living in my own movie. The movie of my life. The leading performer in Vegas who I idolized was Lady Gaga, who had performed her show "Enigma." Her voice, her outfits, her smile, and her performances are all things I idolized. I often thought I could be a Persian version of her.

I considered myself an enigma. From being raised in ultra-conservative Iran and in the relatively conservative small town of Lubbock to the big city of Dallas, while later living in Berkley, I realized how my life is a contrast of extremes. Although I was raised conservatively, I was beginning to grow and wanted to experience more in life.

My parents never held me back and only supported me in my endeavors. I'm an only child, and my parents put all they could in me. But I had to leave Dallas; it was stifling, and I wanted more out of my youth than following the traditional route of going to school, getting a degree, and finding a job. After my problems affording UCLA, I put my academic endeavors on hold.

As I was walking the strip, I found a trash can and threw away all my mental health prescription drugs. I felt they were unnecessary and they were stifling my creativity.

Soon after settling in with my friends, I found a job at a Hooters restaurant. I thought it would be a good job as I was watching girls post on Instagram and TikTok and go viral. They were going viral for being beautiful and funny. However,

I wanted to go viral for my singing. Plus it was a good-paying job, so it was a good fit.

At first, I didn't like the uniforms, but as I worked, I got used to the routine. A guy walks in, checks me out, and tips well. Rinse, repeat, and move forward. I was focused on one thing: becoming a better singer.

As I felt my medications wear off, I started to feel uneasy. I was hallucinating. I didn't know what was happening. I felt as though the lights were starting to dim, the noises of the slot machines and the televisions were beginning to become overwhelming, and I would hear voices that were only in my head. But I still needed to work. I felt like I was in a different level of a dream state, such as in the movie "Inception," and would hear the voices of a train, thinking there was a way out of my constant delusions and hallucination episodes. I heard voices from songs like "you're going to bury me." I also watched movies and television shows at the time, and watched them with my troubled state of mind; I would believe that I was a character from the movie I was watching.

I would party and go out with friends like any other 21-year-old, but I thought I could control it. As I was so focused on my goal of becoming a better singer, I was ignoring any bad feeling or hallucination I experienced. I didn't want anything to hold me back. I pushed forward, worked hard every day, and saved what money I was earning while making connections in the local music scene.

I met a man named Richard, who was very kind and wanted to help me pursue my music career. Richard connected me to a DJ and wanted to help me become the "Queen of Hearts" of Las Vegas. I felt like it was a variation of a theme from Lady Gaga's "Poker Face" song and original, plus I was in Vegas so it was fitting. I continued to work and seek connections while working with voice coaches, and planing out how to perform in venues in and around the Las Vegas area.

Like any other single 21-year-old, I also wanted to find someone to connect with on a romantic level. The Covid-19 shutdown destroyed my social life. Until Las Vegas, I had not consistently connected with my friends for over a year. I was stuck at home like everyone else in the country. But now I was finally free, so I wanted to live life on my terms. No pandemic was going to stop me. I hopped on all the usual dating apps, Tinder, Bumble, Hinge, and Plenty of Fish to meet new people.

I started meeting different men through the apps and it was exciting. I thought, "Maybe I'll meet a famous person or someone who has made it in music or entertainment." The potential of possibilities seemed endless. Las Vegas is such a vibrant city with people seeking a good time. It was alluring to me as it was the exact opposite of what I was raised in. It was the enigma I was seeking.

As I met men on the dating apps, I ended up finding the exact opposite of what I was seeking. I found that many of the men I was meeting were boring or not in touch. Therefore, I struggled to connect with them or to even have a conversation.

Was it them or was it me? I didn't feel good about anything.

I found that many of the men I was meeting only wanted sex. It made me think that maybe I wasn't enough for them. Was I not intriguing enough to stimulate their minds? I began to feel the medications I was taking only a couple of weeks before coming to Vegas completely wear off. I felt more, but I also felt something scary to me at the time: I was losing more control.

As I was feverishly, like an addict, swiping right and left on the apps, I grew antsy. I felt as though I could not find the right person to connect with. I started to lower who I was swiping right on to see if I could find a connection that way. My mind was racing; I was feeling uneasy. I began to spiral. The blurs of faces on the dating apps were meaningless. Yet I still kept swiping. I kept going on meaningless dates.

I started drinking more. I needed something to make me feel better about myself. I was drinking heavily by this point. The first thing I would drink in the morning was a White Claw for breakfast. I needed something to make me feel better about myself and make me forget.

I thought that maybe it wasn't the guy's problem; but instead I was the problem. Maybe I was a boring person. Maybe I wasn't attractive enough. All my insecurities came at once and would then suddenly leave. I did not understand why I felt these extremes. I could not control my feelings. I would endure sudden panic attacks that

I could not control. I couldn't hold back the emotions. I would sometimes break down and cry in the bathroom at work. I would get severely depressed, but would then later feel extremely happy and invincible or on top of the world. My mind was constantly racing.

Trying to find a positive spin, I thought I was in good company as many artists struggle with mental health issues. Artists such as Demi Lovato have openly discussed their struggles with bipolar disorder. I didn't know it then, but I was experiencing extreme and uncontrollable ups and downs. I regretted throwing away my medications. My father would call me every day to ensure I was taking them. I would lie to him and act like I was taking my medication, but I was not. And then it happened. I swiped on the man who would later change the trajectory of my life.

A day in March of 2022

"Ting" "POF: Someone likes you!" read on my locked phone screen. I decided this was the guy. I was going to give my all to him. I would give him what I thought all the other men I encountered on these apps wanted: Sex.

I had my Snapchat handle on my profile, and after connecting on Plenty of Fish, my date connected with me on Snapchat. I was ready to go out. I was seeking fulfillment. I posted on my Snapchat story that I was open to hanging out with anyone to explore what Las Vegas had to offer. I was working a lot, so I needed a release. My mind was not in the right state, so I was seeking an escape.

He responded to my Snapchat story and said that he wanted to hang out. I was bored of dating and talking about nothing. It felt like I was stuck in one Seinfeld episode after another. It seemed as though my conversations went nowhere when I went out on dates.

I responded with what I thought he wanted, "Are you down to get a hotel room, smoke, and fuck?" I thought this would hasten the connection with him. I went into details about using sex toys, domination and being tied up. He seemed excited to try out female domination. We moved our conversation from Snapchat to text messaging one another. I told him where I lived and to pick me up tonight.

As I entered his car, it felt awkward. I knew this was dangerous, but it was exciting at the same time. I started to feel a high. Euphoria. I was on top of the world. I started to feel like I was living again.

In reality, I now know that I was scared. I was terrified of what I was doing. My parents did not raise me this way. I was rebelling. I was doing what I thought was going to make me and the person I was meeting happy. It could have been any person, I simply just wanted to feel accepted. I needed to escape.

I remember feeling as though I was out of my body watching myself in a movie. I was a star for him. He seemed to be interested in me. He started by asking where I was from and was intrigued by the fact that, as a child, I had grown up in Iran. I was the enigma to him. I intrigued him.

Suddenly things changed, and he started mocking that I was from Iran and had to wear a hijab. It took me down hard. I started to feel as though I was drowning. I could not breathe. I was hyperventilating. I didn't want to weird him out, so I controlled it. At the time I also heard a song on the radio that reminded me a lot of the sexual trauma I experienced only a few years back. A strong mix of feelings came over me and the song reminded me of my past. I was having a flashback.

I usually find solace in music. At the time, I was listening to a lot of different artists with imagery. One of the artists I was listening to was MXMS. She used bold imagery and lyrics. It was Gravedigger by MXMS, the sng I was listening to. Everything I wanted to be. Everything I felt I wasn't. I would listen to her songs on repeat on YouTube, studying and obsessing over every detail of imagery she used in her music videos and lyrics. She was dark. She spoke to the dark side of my soul. She spoke to my depression. I remembered parts from her song, some parts were hazy. Not sure if I got all the parts verbatim.

"I play with fire

Don't play with me I got the power

I'm a gravedigger

I'm a, I'm a death-hunter

I'm a, I'm a gravedigger

I'm a, I'm a death-hunter"

This kept repeating in my head as we drove to the hotel together. I couldn't control it. My mind was racing, the elation I was feeling was turning to darkness. I didn't know what else to do but to continue on the date.

"Devil dance calls on me

I swim in imagination

Black on my eyes

I'm cold as a snake

I'm immortal, beautiful, and powerful

Mirror can't capture all."

I felt bad about myself. I felt bad that he was making fun of my heritage. With all the things many think wrong with Iran, I was still born there. I absolutely love America. It's my home, not Iran. Iran's rich culture, mixed with living in the freedoms of the United States, made me who I am. I'm an enigma. So why didn't he accept me?

I am so grateful for living in America. It's who I am now. I hated that I felt disrespected. I am American and completely identify as American. Even though I am Persian, I don't tell people I'm Persian-American. I'm not a hyphenated person. I am American. I hated that he brought up the hijab. I had resisted wearing it as a child. I hated the control. I hated the need to do that to be considered a good person. All of this boiled up in my mind until I began to project the hate onto him.

"I'm the queen motherfucker

Got my crown and my thorns

Blood like wine

It's not a secret

You wanna fuck me

And you'll always remember it"

As the drive continued, I felt I was leaving my body. I was going into full manic mode. I didn't want him to see my instability. I didn't want him to think I was weird. I stayed quiet while he continued to mock me, but his words were piercing. I was sad that I couldn't be normal. Is that all he saw in me? All of my insecurities about myself started to rush in my head. I didn't like myself. I hated myself because I wasn't normal to him.

Why did he only see me as some weirdo from Iran? It was over. I was in full Grave Digger mode. I had no control, I couldn't stop my thoughts. I was out of my body looking at myself. It was not me at this point. I still don't know how best to describe the experience, although losing ones mind feels like the best description. I tried to get a hold of my thoughts:

"I'm a gravedigger

At once

I'm a, I'm a death-hunter

I'm a, I'm a gravedigger

At once

I dig

I dig."

As we exited his vehicle, I was about to run away. That was until I quickly realized that I'm in a place in Las Vegas which I'd never been to before and had no idea where to run to. Thinking to tell myself, I was out of my mind. I could sense something down inside of me that was trying to tell myself not to go with him. "Run! Run! Run! Run away, Nika! Run!" "Your parents would be so disappointed." "All they did was love you." "You are an intelligent and beautiful soul." Don't do it!!" "This isn't who you are!!!" "STOP!"

But I couldn't hold on to any of it. I couldn't control it. All I could think about was the sadness he made me feel. I remember almost bolting as we walked to the hotel lobby. I didn't know what to do. I felt trapped. I felt like I couldn't stop myself. I couldn't control it. I was feeling extremely low. I still did not want him to think I was crazy. He already thought I was weird because I had to wear a hijab in a country I do not know anymore. I spent most of my life growing up in America.

I didn't want to feel down again. However, I could clearly see he was happy about this encounter. He wanted what I thought all men wanted. This was a fantasy. Not my fantasy, but his. I was not there anymore. I was no longer in control.

"I live in a cave

I hear an amber alert

I come out and live your body

I'm immortal motherfucker

I'm a gravedigger

At once

I'm a, I'm a death-hunter

I'm a, I'm a gravedigger"

Checking-In to Hotel

While checking in at the hotel lobby, I saw a woman and heard her say, "I bet she is gonna slit his throat during sex." I'm sure this didn't actually happen, but it's what I was seeing and hearing at the time. Looking back now, I know I was hallucinating.

I was looking at myself as if watching an actress in a thriller movie. For part of me this was exciting. This made me feel good. I kept vacillating between being low and being excited. I was spiraling. I felt nauseous. I felt sick.

I looked at my phone and saw an Amber Alert reading, "Do it." "Do what?!" I thought? I was peering over my own shoulder, looking at my phone screen. It wasn't me. I was a character in a movie. "They are looking for you. They are going to find you." I thought it said on my screen. I was completely out of it.

I was in a full-on manic episode while checking in at the hotel. I believed the people at the slot machines were putting money in and betting on what would happen at the hotel that night. Since he made fun of me coming from Iran, I felt as though some people would bet that I would take revenge on him. People had bags stating, "Take a bet on me," which worsened my delusions further. I was racing. I was trying to control my breathing. I saw a man wearing a shirt reading "Warning!" I thought that was a hint of what was going to happen that night.

All of my delusions, both visual and auditory hallucinations, made me lose my mind. Las Vegas is beautiful, but it's overwhelming at the same time. The nature of Red Rock Canyon and other places are such an escape from the Strip with visitors, lights, and non-stop action. I wanted to escape.

When we arrived at the hotel room, I felt cold, empty, and dark. I suggested he should grab some alcohol and orange juice from downstairs. When he went downstairs, I started to take off my clothes. I looked in the mirror and thought, this actress is hot. I started to dance like Selma Hayek from *Dusk Till Dawn*. I felt powerful. She was so pretty. She controlled the entire room in that dance scene. I felt as though that's who I was watching. I was transforming into Selma with the Gravedigger song playing on repeat in my head. I was hallousinating a snake around my shoulders just like the dance scene from the movie. He was George Clooney, but I was going to win, not him.

He then came back with a bottle of tequila and orange juice. I started to take shots. I didn't care what was in my drink. I needed something to make me feel good. I wasn't there. The character was breaking. I needed it to keep it going. I showered first, and then he also took one. When he came out of the shower I was already in bed with a towel around me. He asked me, "Would you like the lights on or off?" I responded with "off," so he turned off the lights.

We started to kiss. It was horrible. I didn't want to do it, but it wasn't me; I was hallucinating. "Keep acting. You're in control, not him." I took off his glasses, and asked if he wanted me to put the red blindfold on him. He wanted pain and pleasure just like in the *Dusk Till Dawn* scene. It was a fantasy. We had already discussed this.

Selma lured everyone with her powerful sexuality. She owned the room. All those men in the scene wanted her. She owned them with her beauty, and her power; she was in control. My character was owning him. My character was powerful. I was Selma. I hopped on him, but the condom kept slipping off. We started to have intercourse. He was mine. I have him now.

"Everybody wants hotness but they don't pay the price

Nothing going to stop me

'Til the amber alert drops

I'm a gravedigger

I'm a, I'm a death-hunter

I'm a, I'm a gravedigger

Fire surrounds me

I'm a death-hunter

Play fire with me

I'm a, I'm a gravedigger

I'm a, I'm a death-hunter

At once"

    Selma took a room filled with men apart in *Dusk Till Dawn* before George Clooney killed her with the chandelier. I then grabbed a knife that I had kept in my purse. I didn't know what to do. It was in my head. He wanted it. I don't want to hurt this person, but at the same time he had expressed the desire to feel pain during our sexual interaction. It was like a movie scene. He was blindfolded.

We had discussed sexual pleasure from domination, pain and role-playing. Although it was all in my head. A fantasy was now coming into reality. I was inebriated and in a manic state at this point. The real me did not want to hurt him, as a voice was telling me to run out of the room and leave the situation. But we had already engaged in sexual gratification.

He quickly takes the blindfold off and starts choking me hard and yelling "What are you doing?!?" I began to panic. I was hyperventilating. I couldn't control myself. This isn't real. I said "sorry" and ran out of the room naked with a butt plug inside of me.

Chapter 6:

Custody Scene

I was panicking. I did not know what was going on. I ran from the room to the staircase of the hotel and called 911. Even though I called 911, the phone only connected me with the hotel lobby. They asked me what happened and which floor and room I was in. I could not remember. There was blood on my arms. What did I do? My neck hurts. Why did he choke me? He wanted this. We texted and had conversations about this. We discussed what we were going to do. He did everything to facilitate our meeting. I was giving him what he wanted. I don't want to be a weirdo, a conservative girl who wasn't open to trying new things.

But, Why?

Soon afterward, a hotel security guard came. He asked why? I said for revenge. I was a character in the TV show *Homeland* now. The revenge was because I felt like he used me. He took advantage of me. He stole something from me. I wasn't in my mind. I didn't know what to say. I didn't think anything was real.   It was all a movie. I was Carrie from *Homeland*.

I wore a jacket that day with an American flag and thought to myself how I would love to work in the U.S. government. I loved America and *Homeland* was such a great show. I've always had the goal of being a lawyer. I did debate all through high school and college for this one scene. I was a nerd. I endured all the mockery to blossom into the person I am at this moment. I was reborn in this scene, but it was a nightmare. All I had to do was turn off the TV to make everything go back to normal, but it still wouldn't go away. Everything was a haze. It was surreal.

Interrogation scene

The hotel security returned, but this time with a bedsheet so I could cover myself. They told me that the police were on their way. After some time, two police officers arrived and they took me to the back of the closet area to sit me at a table. I asked several times to get my clothes or to remove the butt plug that was still in me. However, they seemed more concerned with detaining me than actually hearing what I was asking. They treated me as though they wanted me to stay in character.

One of the officers was very attractive. He had dreamy blue eyes, was tall, and very fit. He looked as though he had been cast for a movie role. He looked like a movie star. The two officers asked me some questions and it remained an out-of-body experience. My mouth was moving, but I could not comprehend or control what I was saying. All I could hear was a high-pitched tone as I watched my half-naked self sitting across from the two police officers. It was a great scene, but what was I saying? What were they asking?

One of the police officers looked alarmed at my answers. His facial expressions were the perfect reactions an actor would portray in a movie scene. But then again, they seemed to be too real. I was getting uncomfortable again. "Why wasn't he breaking the scene?" "What did I do?" "Did they see my breasts?" "Did one slip out?" "Did I read my lines wrong?" "What was I saying?" "What did he say?" I kept asking them if I could put on some clothes and take five from the scene. I had this butt plug in me from the other scene and I needed it out.

It was getting even more uncomfortable. I wanted to run; I was feeling hot. But I couldn't let them see my anxiety attacks, I wouldn't get the acting job. I wanted to take off my sheet and just run out. I started having flashbacks of being in Iran and being questioned by the Morality Police. I remember this scene. "Wait, I've done this before!" I started to have an uncontrollable feeling of darkness and started to have tunnel vision while feeling nauseated all at once. "I'm losing it!" I'm losing it!" "Get ahold of yourself Nika!" Stay in character.

In my head, I'm back in Iran as a seven-year-old being detained by the Morality Police and they are harassing me for not wearing the hijab. They are mocking me. They are making me feel bad about myself. But why? I didn't like the hijab because it was too hot. I wanted to be free.

Being naked in front of these officers is nothing compared to what I remember as a child. I understand that now. I wasn't in a scene. This was my real life. I didn't understand anything that was happening at that moment. To this day, watching the tapes of myself, I don't see myself. I see someone else. Someone hurting. Someone so scared. Someone traumatized. Someone who was not in their right mind.

After what seemed like forever, two other detective-looking men showed up.

Custody Scene

They were dressed up in suits and wearing hats. They looked so serious. This was a great scene. I wanted to see what happens next. They started to ask me questions and I was watching my mouth move, but I did not understand what I was saying. I was so calm on the outside, but was panicking inside. As I responded, all I could hear was the same high-pitched sound. I still couldn't make out what they were saying. I didn't know what I was saying.

I later discovered that these serious looking men were Homeland Security. Was I changing roles? Am I a CIA spy for the U.S.? What's going on here? Was I Clair Danes in *Homeland* again? Am I supposed to role-play her now? I'm feeling manic. I don't know what to do. "Where is this show going?" I was nauseous. I did not like the way the men were staring at me. I was feeling bad about myself. I didn't even know what I had done wrong.

Suddenly I felt the cold handcuffs slap on my wrists, and all of these men were walking me out of the hotel. It was cold. I entered the back of the police car and began shivering. It still feels like everything is unreal and I'm playing a part in a movie. It was all so surreal and the feelings of conflict I had at that time were overwhelmingly confusing.

Jail Experience

As I arrived at the Henderson Jail everyone I encountered was staring at me. It was similar to the scene just a few moments ago when I was walking into the hotel casino and was hallucinating. The

Custody Scene

first lady wouldn't stop looking at me and asked, "Your name?" "These are your possessions." "Please wear this at all times and do not try to take it off," she said in a monotone voice. I was given a green suicide blanket that was required to be worn at all times. A scarlet letter to everyone in the facility that I was on suicide watch. I was alone. I felt dirty immediately upon walking into the jail. Officers in different uniforms escorted me to my cell. I was in a solitary cell. It was cold. It was filthy. There was no pillow, no blanket. It was soulless. I started to feel the darkest feelings of despair I have ever felt in my short life.

I had to try to sleep on concrete with the light blaring in my face in a very cold, and moldy room. There was no soap. There was no toilet paper. I was so scared that I began crying uncontrollably in my cell.

The feelings of despair and loneliness I felt in that moment, are feelings I would not wish on any human being.

I didn't know if my parents knew where I was or if anyone cared for me. I asked one of the officers if she had any advice, and she suggested calling bail bond companies and asking them to reach out to my parents. I then called numerous bail bond companies, to which all I heard was: "We can't help you. Click." Most bond companies did not want to manage a high profile inmate. Most ignored my requests until I reached one that was nice enough to at least call my parents for me.

A day later, an officer tells me that I've got a call from my attorney, so I proceed to a dangling phone. On the other end I hear a lady saying that my parents have hired them as my attorney and that I will soon be going to court for a hearing to determine my bail amount.

I was so nervous and scared to see my parents. The feeling of shame was worse than when I kept my sexual trauma from them. I couldn't escape it. It gripped my entire body. I felt so bad about myself. It wasn't who they raised. I wasn't the person they invested so much into. I was someone else at that moment. Something I did not like. Something I couldn't escape.

I wanted to cry when the prosecutor asked for an initial two hundred thousand dollars bail. I could see the sadness overcome my father's face and the grief in his eyes. I felt so ashamed. I felt so worthless.

After my lawyer asked for a lower bail amount, I was so grateful that the judge agreed to a rate of sixty thousand dollars, but at the same time all I could think of was the equivalent cost of my last year at UCLA. It felt like I just threw my life away. I understand why they had me on suicide watch now. I understood my scarlet letter. How could I ever redeem myself from this? I couldn't control my feelings of shame. I had disappointed my parents. I was extremely depressed and low. I never wanted to do this to them. I didn't want to live any more.

After my bail hearing, I returned to my jail cell and saw a "dangerous tendencies" note beside my name. I hadn't done anything in jail that might have provoked the officers, but I supposed the attempted murder charge was also not a petty crime. Did they see how depressed and ashamed

I was? When the whole scenario went down, I didn't know what was going on. Despite this, I still felt ashamed.

The following day I was told I would be moving to Clark County Detention Center since I was charged with felony-level charges. I cooperated with all the instructions I was given, but I remember the same dark feelings and out of body experience while being questioned by the Morality police and Homeland Security detectives. Watching my mouth move, but only hearing the same deafening high-pitched sound ringing in my ears.

On the car ride from Henderson to CCDC, I met someone, who later became a friend, who said she had experienced jail. She told me numerous interesting stories about jail and gave advice on coping during my time there. When we arrived at CCDC, I had to go through multiple screenings and questionnaires. I was later confined to a larger jail cell with seven other girls. It was so cold, but there was at least soap and toilet paper here. The food was terrible. I felt like an animal eating table scraps. I was so desperately hungry all of the time. I wanted to eat but nothing tasted good. I still felt so bad. Everything tasted worse than normal and jail food was already as bad as it could get.

After two days, I was given jail clothing and moved to a different cell. By this point, I hadn't showered in a week and felt and smelled disgusting. My depression was getting worse. My low was even lower. I didn't know how much lower I could reach. I was still declining.

Even after moving to the general population, I still had difficulties adjusting. I already had a reputation before going to jail, as everyone knew about my case. My story was all over the news and I saw a fellow inmate reading a newspaper where I was on the front page. She stopped and stared at me like I was going to kill her. Some girls were scared of me. Many of my fellow inmates avoided me. I was a high profile inmate. Everyone knew. There was no escaping it. I felt even lower again.

My parents were unaware of the jail conditions, and neither of them or myself knew how to communicate with one another. I had no money in my commissary account, so I had to trade my disgusting food with other girls for shampoo and soap just to get a decent shower. I felt so dirty. But I couldn't escape it. I had a jail cellmate who was very friendly to me. Her name was Queen Kayda. We both had musical aspirations and it was interesting to me to discuss both of our goals and ambitions in music.

My attorney visited me after two weeks, and I finally was able to request money to be added to my commissary account so I could call my parents and purchase products like snacks, shampoo, and drawing materials. My attorney also informed me that since I would be going through a competency hearing, I would need to stay in jail for longer despite my bond having been posted. I was too depressed to understand any of it.

I stayed in jail for a total of six weeks. These six weeks were the most miserable and brutal six weeks of my life. My depression had progressively gotten lower each day during that time.

I felt as if the guards treated me like an animal, and there was no remorse for being mean to me. Being strip-searched at random times completely took away any humanity, privacy and dignity. I had a couple of different roommates in my jail cell. They were an escape from the dark reality I was experiencing. I had to make the best out of my situation. After getting some money in my commissary from my parents, I purchased some card games. I would play countless games with my cell roommates or would continuously play solitary to make time pass by. I would read books and even began to write this very book. What I saw on TV and the internet was not me. YouTubers would speculate, the media wrote stories that were far from the truth, and I needed an outlet.

Singing was my other outlet. It made me happy, if just for a moment. A vital moment of escape from the darkness and despair I couldn't escape. I would sing in my jail cell and those fellow inmates around me commented on how beautiful my voice was. One joked that I was the general population's radio station. I would take requests from fellow inmates and would sing the songs they asked. I would sing songs from some kid classics such as the Little Mermaid or Anastasia.

I still had the goal of becoming a singer, and I would focus on it while I was in my jail cell. I created a plan for when I would get out to pursue my dreams in music. I even started writing songs and practicing them while serving my time.

The day finally came. I was told that I would be released from jail. I was thrilled. I gave away all my snacks to the girls who didn't get the opportunity to get out of jail. Even though I packed up my stuff and was ready to leave, there was still a lengthy process on my release. I had to wait in a different unit for six hours before being freed. I told my parents I would be released that day, but I had no accurate timing on when I would actually get out.

I felt joy stepping outside the jail and seeing my father waiting for me. He had been waiting for over six hours. When he walked toward me, I could tell there was something wrong with his leg, which I would later find out was because of the stress and nerves I had caused him when the news broke out. I felt delighted to finally be back with my dad, but also petrified and terrified of what was to come. I felt like an outsider to the free world. I remember my dad telling me not to Google myself as he handed me a phone. I couldn't help it. I went straight to the bathroom once home and Googled myself.

Seeing my mug shot and all the nasty hate comments people put on my social media and online made me cry. How could I be such a disappointment? But, also, why is half of what is in the media a bunch of lies? Some say I am a "Russian spy," and other websites reported complete misinformation about who I was. I was disgusted by the speculation I saw on social media. I was even nervous about giving out my name the first time I ordered food out of jail, believing they would think I'm that "crazy girl" they've read about in the newspapers. I was depressed, but at the same time happy to be out of jail and reunited with my family.

Chapter 7:

Moving forward

Arriving home in Dallas had a nostalgic feeling that I can't describe. Being back at home, in my bed, with my parents, was a happiness I hoped to keep forever. Tasting my mom's home cooked food was like food for both my body and soul.

Although I was thrilled to be back home, I could see the sadness in the eyes of my parents. The absolute disappointment was something I could not escape. I was told stories of how they reacted when they heard the news, which broke my heart. Why would I do something to put my parents through something like this?

Music Career

I still had my goals in mind. I signed with a record studio for the very first time. I was so excited and thrilled to record at a professional music studio. I recorded several cover songs and was starting to rebuild my self-esteem. I was proud of getting over part of my depression and getting out there to create something. I was still believing in myself and doing what I could to attain the goals and dreams I had. My life didn't feel as ruined when I was singing. I felt alive. I felt as though I was fulfilling my purpose.

As a condition of my bail, I was put under house arrest, so I was limited in where I could go. I was allowed to work, and was able to gain employment at a local restaurant as a server. Given my circumstances, I was beyond happy that I was even able to have the chance at a job. At the time, I had no idea, but my employers knew all about my pending charges and decided to give me a chance anyway. I am forever grateful for them believing in me and not assuming the worst in me like so many people did. They understood what I was going through; they were not in the bedroom. They didn't believe the media. They did not know how vulnerable I was in that hotel room in Las Vegas.

I lost a lot of my so-called friends. It was isolating and depressing. Going on social media such as Facebook and reading hate comments from high school friends was something that I found very hard to deal with, but I also found that in the larger picture, I was able to figure out who my real friends were.

I am so grateful for the close friends like Lauren and Skyler who always believed in me and supported me throughout this whole ordeal and supported my music endeavors.

When serving time in jail, I was planning to produce a music video, so I connected with a music producer from a local Dallas studio. They did not judge me. Instead they were excited to work with me on my "Spaceman" music video.

Shooting the music video took sixteen hours at six different locations all over the DFW area. The video featured numerous local influencers and dancers from the Dallas area. Creating my first music video was an exhausting yet rewarding experience.

Later on, the local media began to hear about concerts I was holding and portrayed it as a scandal as I was on house arrest. This was far from the truth. I had already made sure to contact both my attorney and the GPS tracking company to ensure I was not in violation of the rules set forth in my house arrest or bail.

I was so grateful for everyone who helped in the production of my music video. I was proud that despite the impending serious charges I was facing, I had put my mind to creating and producing a professional level music video. My video ended up going viral on YouTube, receiving over a hundred thousand views. Like any artist, I was just happy that people enjoyed something I created.

I also had the opportunity to record my first EP album entitled "Spaceman." I'm so proud of this project. I spent so much time in the studio recording and working with some of the best music engineers in the Dallas area. My parents were also very proud of my work. Despite all that had happened, it meant so much that I was able to make them smile at my concert.

I hosted several concerts in Denton featuring myself and other artists. In my life, I've only been to a few concerts, and it felt exciting to finally host my very own concerts to bring joy and entertainment to others. I sold out of all VIP tickets and played to a packed room at my first ever concert. I felt like a true artist. The venue loved the crowd which turned out and I felt like I was finally moving in the right direction. However, the headlines hit again and I found myself on the first story of the local news.

Chapter 8:

Why did it happen again?

I was sitting in one of my classes at the University of Texas at Dallas. It was not my dream school, but it was an opportunity and a good school. I wanted to continue my studies and complete my final hours to obtain my bachelor's degree. If I was going to wait a long time before my case was resolved, I wanted to continue to progress and better myself in the process. While working long hours as a server, attending college and planning and producing music, I wanted to live life to its fullest. I had no idea what the future held for me, but I was free to express and better myself if only for a short time.

In addition to school, I was producing music and holding concerts at the time. The profits from all concerts I held benefited the Iranian Women's Foundation. It was a creative escape while helping a cause that is personally dear to me. With all that is happening in Iran, I wanted to help girls like myself who are living in the country. I want to help those girls having to deal with the problems associated with a regime that takes brutal control to maintain its power. I lived there, so I felt compelled to do something to help. I did not want to be on TV for anything other than helping others and creating music that people enjoyed. People said mean things. They judge me for my pending charges.

I never planned on being in the media in that way for a second time. My story spread even further. I was all over the news again. I didn't like this attention, in fact I wanted to escape it forever. I didn't want to feel bad again. People were saying so many mean things about me.

I had to endure several hearings at UTD and was removed while attending a class. I didn't want to be kicked out of school. I was just trying to move forward. I never wanted to hurt anyone. I hated when the campus police came to escort me out of my classroom. I felt ashamed. I really didn't want this kind of attention. All I wanted was to live my life and finish school.

Chapter 9:
Future Plans/ Conclusion

The things that happen in our lives shape us. And the things that happened in my past made me into the person I am today. A strong, intelligent woman. But I am also an enigma. I am a girl who needs and is receiving help. I regularly see a psychiatrist and am on more specialized mental health medications.

I want to be free from the sexual trauma I experienced, I want to be free of the experiences I endured as a young girl mocked by the Morality Police for not wearing a hijab; I want to be free of the headlines designed to sell papers rather than cover the truth. I am forever grateful that I was given a second chance. A chance to prove to the world that I can be a successful member of society. One that is able to make a positive contribution. One that is able to show the world that there should be more open discussions of mental health and openness to a more sympathetic society.

I'm not a victim. I'm not writing this for sympathy. I'm not writing this because I think I need the attention. I'm writing this for all the girls like me. The girls who struggle with being accepted. The girls who have low self-esteem. The girls who struggle with their body image and weight. The girls who, for whatever reason, felt as though they were less than. The girls who are bullied on social media. I do this for them and to tell my real story. The one the media and whatever sound bite won't allow to be told. All of these opposites and layers are who I am. I am an enigma.

Printed in the USA
CPSIA information can be obtained
at www.ICGtesting.com
LVHW020251051023
760125LV00004B/437